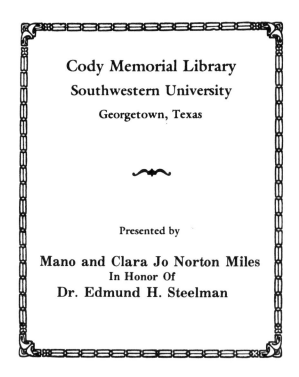

Archaeology

Figurines found at an archaeological site in
the ancient land of Mesopotamia.

Archaeology

by Denise Schmandt-Besserat

Steck-Vaughn Company
An Intext *Publisher*
Austin, Texas

Because of the many books we have shared, this book is
dedicated to my children, Alex, Chris, and Phillip.

Steck-Vaughn's Wings Books Series introduces a
wide range of concepts in science and social studies
to students in the middle grades. The books in the
Series include thought-provoking questions and dem-
onstrations that will encourage readers to find out
more about the various subjects.

Library of Congress Cataloging in Publication Data

Schmandt-Besserat, Denise.
  Archaeology.

  (Wings books series)
  Summary: Text and photographs introduce the methods used by
archaeologists and explain how the artifacts found fit together like
puzzle pieces to reveal life of long ago.
  1. Archaeology—Juvenile literature. [1. Archaeology] I. Title.
CC80.S35   913'.031   73-11275
ISBN 0-8114-7757-6

Introduction

Archaeology (are-ki-<u>ol</u>-uh-ji) may be defined as the study of the people, customs, and life of ancient times. The word comes to us from the Greek words <u>arkhaios</u>, meaning ancient, and <u>logos</u>, meaning study. Archaeologists try to find answers to questions like the following: What did early people look like? And how did they adapt to the environment? Where were the first cities built? Who invented writing? How did our industrialized civilization come about?

Tools, coins, written documents, and traces of architecture are artifacts (<u>are</u>-ti-facts), man-made objects, that can help answer these questions. The artifacts, as well as food remains and bones that archaeologists find, are like pieces of a puzzle. They can be fitted together to depict life of long ago.

By studying early people and ancient civilizations, archaeologists make exciting discoveries. But many questions remain unanswered.

Is it important to find out what has happened across the wide gap of time? What bond exists between you and the hunter who sat beside a campfire 300,000 years ago? Will knowing how human beings developed from hunter to today's city dweller help us in better understanding ourselves and the world we live in?

Texas Archeological Research Laboratory,
The University of Texas at Austin

Archaeologists carefully uncover skeletons. The skeletons reveal the stature
of early man. Tools and weapons were found with the skeletons at this site
and are indicative of the way of life and the degree of technology achieved
by the culture to which they belong. Among the objects found at this site
were: (1) a conch shell container, flint blades, red pigment, perforated discs
for ear ornaments, a beaver tooth, bone hairpins, a small effigy pipe, and a
grinding stone; (2) arrowheads, flint blades, and gray pigment; (3) polished
celts (ancient implements shaped like chisels).

Texas Archeological Survey,
The University of Texas at Austin

ROCK-SHELTER AND CAVE SITES. Have you ever seen a cave or rock-shelter and thought what a safe shelter it would be? Early man found that such a location provided a natural roof against rain and cold winds, as well as a refuge against wild animals. Cave and rock-shelter sites are usually well preserved, as they have not been destroyed by the plough or natural erosion.

Where do archaeologists find ancient remains?

To study ancient cultures, the various stages of human beings' development, archaeologists must first find an area where well-preserved material from the people and the period interested in can be found. A place where ancient remains are found is called an "archaeological site." The size of sites can vary from that of modest camp-fires once used by hunters to that of large buried cities covering acres of land. The date of sites can range from the very beginning of mankind some 3,000,000 years ago to more recent times. There are many kinds of sites.

1

Sites are often found accidentally. A bulldozer may uncover traces of ancient architecture when clearing land for a highway. Farmers have unearthed stone tools or opened a burial site while ploughing their fields. However, archaeologists do not leave the discovery of sites to chance. They organize surveys or careful studies of areas that were likely to have attracted settlements by man. Such areas would have had game and food resources, natural shelters, and abundant water supply.

Archaeologists go over the selected area on foot or by car, looking for clues such as ruins; pottery sherds, or broken pieces of pottery; and tools.

OPEN-AIR SITE. Are there any places near you that might be potential archaeological sites? Remember that water is necessary for all human settlements. What kind of land would early man have looked for as he began to produce his own food? What kind of environment would hunters have needed?

Open-air sites are usually difficult to find because they are often covered by vegetation or by buildings. Many have been destroyed by bulldozers and agricultural machinery.

Texas Archeological Research Laboratory,
The University of Texas at Austin

Roger Agache, Abbeville, France

Left: AERIAL PHOTOGRAPH. In the morning light, the photograph has captured the traces of a complex system of ancient ditches in the recently ploughed fields of Neufmoulin, France.

Below: UNDERWATER SITE. A diver examines the underwater site of a 4th century shipwreck along the coast of Turkey. The depth of the water is 140 feet. What do you think might be found at a shipwreck site?

University of Pennsylvania Museum, Philadelphia

Some archaeological sites can best be detected from a plane. Patterns of different colors appear from a certain height, contrasting with the less fertile parts of the field and pointing out the location and plan of ancient structures, roads, or burial places. The different colors are due to differences in the growth of plants, because vegetation usually grows better where the ancient ditches were dug and where the soil is deeper.

3

A NEAR EASTERN MOUND. The remains of cities contained within mounds have been covered under the sand for thousands of years. Can you see the step trench excavated on the side of Tell Judaidah, Turkey? The step trench provides the archaeologist with a sampling of artifacts from the latest occupation, located at the top of the mound, to the earliest occupation, located at the bottom.

Buried Cities of the Near East

The buried cities of the Near East are sites that are usually easy to detect. They look like gigantic anthills strewn with ancient potsherds, fragments of broken earthen pots. These buried cities are called "mounds" in English, "tells" in Arabic, and "tepes" in one of the Persian languages. Mounds are made up of layers of houses built on top of houses—or cities built on top of other cities.

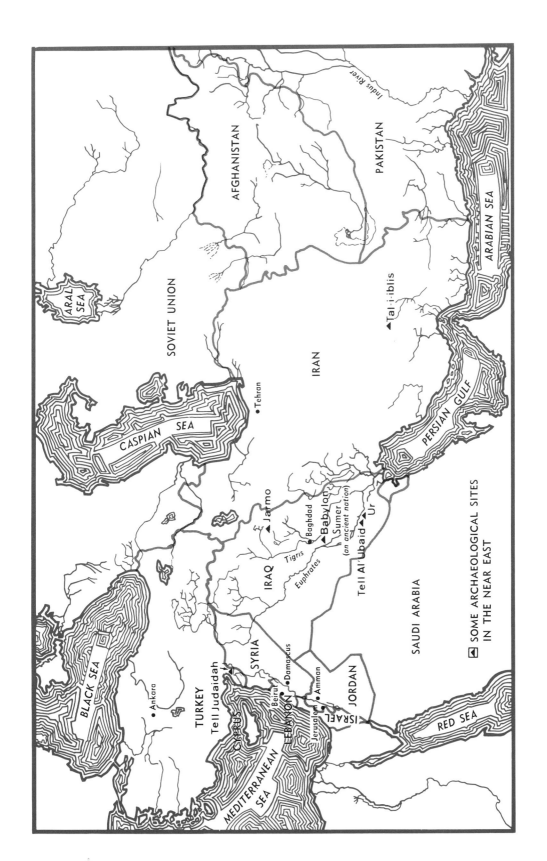

SOME ARCHAEOLOGICAL SITES
IN THE NEAR EAST

5

Stratigraphy

Archaelogists study the stratigraphy (stra-tig-gra-fi) of mounds and other sites, digging into parallel layers, or strata, placed one upon another. Stratigraphy means written in layers and comes from the Latin word stratum (stray-tum), layer, and the Greek word graphein (gray-fain), writing. A search is made in the strata for objects that were long ago buried under dust and sand blown by the wind, that may have been covered with mud carried by rain, or that were hidden by soil produced by the decomposition, or decay, of plants.

AN EXAMPLE OF LAYERS IN SOIL. A layer of topsoil and vegetation approximately ten inches thick covers archaeological material at this site. What is the archaeological material in this picture, and what does it tell you about the environment?

Texas Archeological Survey,
The University of Texas at Austin

BRICKMAKER. In the Near East today, the bricks are made very much in the same way the Sumerians did 5,000 years ago. A square wooden mold is filled with a mixture of dirt and water. The finger marks will help the mortar in adhering. After a few days in the sun, the bricks will become dry and hard.

Five thousand years ago a state called Sumer was located in an area of presentday Iraq. In the dry and barren land between the Tigris (<u>ti</u>-gris) and Euphrates (yoo-<u>fray</u>-teez) rivers, there were no trees or stones. The Sumerians used reeds and river mud for building materials and built their homes with sun-dried bricks. The mud brick or clay houses of the Sumerians did not resist weathering well and did not last long. Once they were degraded, or worn down, the houses were abandoned. When all the walls had collapsed, what remained would be flattened out, and another house would be built on top of the debris of the old one. The surface of the ground, therefore, slowly rose approximately one foot per century.

The Sumerians built what may be the world's first highly developed civilization, but it is only in the last one hundred years that we have learned the story of their many achievements. This "lost civilization" was uncovered by archaeologists.

7

In the Near East, people are still building their houses with mud bricks, and mounds are still growing today. The city of Irbil (ihr -<u>bill</u>) in Iraq is perched at the top of the debris of several ancient cities. Erosion, or the wearing away by the action of water and wind, has smoothed the mounds into gradual slopes or hills.

The task of archaeologists is to extract the ancient artifacts from under the dirt or from under the debris of mud houses. The top layer of dirt and mud is called the "surface layer." As the surface layer is just the product of erosion, it does not usually yield any artifacts. Beneath the surface layer, the ancient remains are spread in a layer called the "archaeological layer, or stratum."

THE CITY OF IRBIL, IRAQ. In this airview of the modern city of Irbil, the mound structure is clearly visible.

The Oriental Institute, the University of Chicago.
Flight provided by I. P. C., Ltd.

A SINGLE ARCHAEOLOGICAL LAYER. The test pit shows a thick layer of shells which are kitchen refuse of an ancient settlement. What do the shells indicate as to how early man depended upon this environment? What food remains would be preserved at a present-day landfill, and what would they tell future generations about our use of the environment today?

The archaeological layer varies in depth with the length of time a site was occupied. In the case of a Sumerian city like Ur (oor), which had been flourishing for thousands of years, the mound reached a height of twenty-four feet and had many layers. A site that had been occupied only a short time would make a layer only a few inches in depth. Such a layer could be made by hunters spending one season in a cave.

9

MULTIPLE ARCHAEOLOGICAL LAYERS. This deep trench shows the building up or accumulation of many layers in a mound.

Some sites were abandoned because of invasion by enemies; the spread of disease, or epidemics; drought and the lack of food; or migration, the movement of a people from one area to another with the seasons. Much later, the sites were reoccupied by different people. Such sites will have two or more superimposed archaelogical layers which must be carefully separated, or isolated, because they yield completely different material and give information about different occupants. This was the case of Ur where the Sumerians had been building their city upon the remains of an ancient settlement of reed huts. The name of the early people who had inhabited the huts is not known. It is known only that most of their tools were made of stone, for metal was still quite rare. The archaeological layers made from the settlement of reed huts are characterized by a great quantity of brightly painted pottery. This pottery is called "Ubaid" (oo-bayd) pottery from the name of the site, Tell Al'Ubaid, where it was first discovered.

RECONSTRUCTION OF A REED HUT. As the reeds have completely disintegrated, we do not know what the Ubaid huts were like. We can imagine, however, that they were similar to the reed huts built today by people of the area. Scattered bricks discovered in the same level tell us that the Ubaid people of Ur also lived in more permanent houses. Excavations at other Ubaidian sites revealed that these early people built not only spacious houses but elaborate temples.

UBAID POTSHERDS. Since its invention, probably around 7000 B. C., pottery has been a common household item, and pieces of pottery are usually found in abundance wherever people have lived. Pottery is a good clue for archaeologists because its texture, color, shape, and decoration tell much about the period of time in which it was made. Archaeologists can often identify the people who lived in a site just by the pottery they left behind. The Ubaid pottery is characterized by its green color and its geometric design of floral motifs painted with a wide brush in black or red paint.

Ubaid pottery contrasts with the plain, beige or red vases used by the Sumerians and found in quantity in their layer. In turn, when the Sumerians were defeated by Babylon around 2000 B.C., their conquerors again rebuilt new cities, thus adding another layer to Ur. This last layer is characterized by a fine white pottery often shaped like elegant footed goblets

Above: SUMERIAN BOWLS. These thick, coarse, porous, and poorly fired bowls are a puzzle to archaeologists, and no one knows exactly how they were used. They were found by the thousands in early Sumerian temples. It is thought they may have been votive bowls for offerings.

Left: BABYLONIAN GOBLET. This pottery is easy to differentiate from the Ubaid and Sumerian. It is a fine, white ware having concentric rings next to the rim. The rings indicate that the goblet was made on the potter's wheel.

13

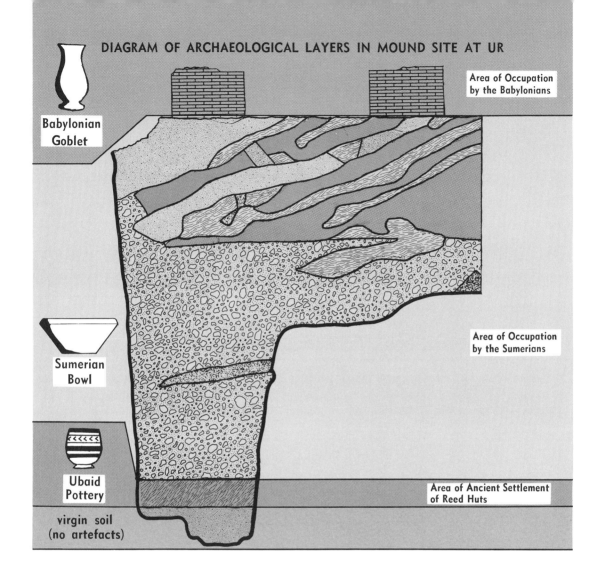

DIAGRAM OF ARCHAEOLOGICAL LAYERS IN MOUND SITE AT UR

Area of Occupation by the Babylonians

Babylonian Goblet

Sumerian Bowl

Area of Occupation by the Sumerians

Ubaid Pottery

Area of Ancient Settlement of Reed Huts

virgin soil (no artefacts)

Reading the Layers

Archaeologists can actually read stratigraphy because each layer has a different composition and appears in a different color. Some layers, probably rich in organic materials such as food remains, are very dark brown or even black. Others which have witnessed the devastation of fire are full of ashes and are gray. Layers with mud-brick architecture appear light beige in color.

Texas Archeological Survey,
The University of Texas at Austin

Texas Archeological Survey,
The University of Texas at Austin

Left: **EXAMPLE OF STRATIGRAPHY.** At this site, the dark archaeological layers alternate with the light-colored layers made by flood sediments which accumulated in periods when the site was abandoned.

Right: **DEEP SOUNDING.** Note how the position of various layers is marked off on the walls of the vertical cut.

When archaeologists begin work at a site they first try to find out the stratigraphy to know how many occupation layers there are. For this purpose they dig a narrow vertical, or upright, trench from the highest point of the site to the virgin or undisturbed soil. This kind of trench is called "deep sounding." The walls of the deep sounding show a complete vertical cut of the site, and the different layers can be distinguished.

The Oriental Institute, University of Chicago

The step trench dug into the Near Eastern mound exposes the different layers. Characteristic objects from each layer retrace for the archaeologist the story of the mound from 600 A.D. to 6000 B.C. Can you identify any of the objects?

1. 600—300 A.D.
2. 300 A.D.—64 B.C.
3. 64—500 B.C.
4. 500—1000 B.C.
5. 1000—1200 B.C.
6. 1200—1600 B.C.
7. 1600—1800 B.C.
8. 1800—2100 B.C.
9. 2100—2400 B.C.
10. 2400—2600 B.C.
11. 2600—2800 B.C.
12. 2800—3100 B.C.
13. 3100—3500 B.C.
14. 4000—6000 B.C.

What do clues found by archaeologists reveal?

When the Sumerians abandoned their old, decayed houses, they left behind all the goods for which they had no more use. Unfortunately, only a small portion of the material has reached us. Look around at your own house and all of the things that are in it. Were a cataclysm to destroy your home, what would remain for archaeologists to find, say 2,000 years from now? What would be left of the following: furniture, carpeting, rugs, clothes, pictures, roof, walls, windowpanes, dishes, food in the refrigerator? What objects do you think might be found and be of interest to archaeologists? What would they tell about you and your family or about the time in which you live?

From the partly corroded metal fragments and partly distorted plastic objects—mixed with the debris of concrete, plaster, stones, bricks, and earthenware—an archaeologist would have a difficult time picturing the atmosphere of your home. Many questions would remain unanswered.

A SCENE IN THE AUTHOR'S HOME. If struck at this moment by a cataclysm, what would remain 2,000 years later with which archaeologists could reconstruct the scene?

1. Stone Wall
2. Bones (5 Human Skeletons and 1 Dog Skeleton)
3. Metal (Window Frame, Doorknob, Ashtray, Goblet, Nails, Watch, Wedding Rings, Sneaker Cleats, Dog Collar)
4. Broken Glass (Window, Picture Frames, Watch)
5. Pottery Sherds (Flowerpots, Coffee Mugs, Vase)
6. Plastic (Doorbell, Electric Switch Plate, Game Tokens)

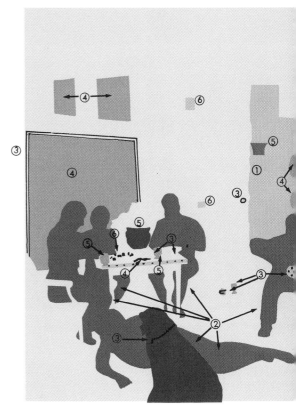

Department of Anthropology, the University of Utah,
Salt Lake City

AN INDIAN BURIAL SITE, MOQUI CANYON, UTAH. The body was placed in a flexed position, and a few vessels were placed beside it. The vessels probably once contained food.

The prehistoric peoples who once lived in the plateau area of the southwestern United States are called "Anasazi" (ah-nuh-*sah*-zi), Basket Makers. The Pueblo Indians of Arizona and New Mexico are their living descendants.

Burial Sites

Belief in an afterlife was held by most ancient people, and in many religions the dead were buried with their possessions in order that they might enjoy them in a future life.

What do you think the clues in this photograph might reveal to archaeologists?

Shipwreck Sites

Ships carried goods to harbors and sailed back with other cargo. When misfortune hit them on their route, ships often sank with their total lading. Can you find a story in this view of a shipwreck?

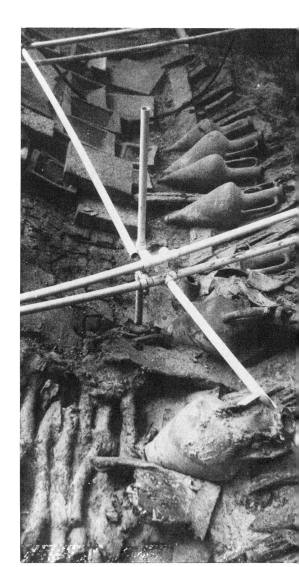

Kyrenia Ship Excavation, Cyprus

SHIPWRECK SITE. The Kyrenia ship in Cyprus. In the foreground is a cargo of roughhewn logs. Beyond stretches the ship's wooden flooring. A load of grain-milling stones lies scattered above it. At the right, a few amphoras (*am*-for-uhs), jars for storing oil, wine, honey, or grain, rest as originally placed against the wooden hull of the ship.

Texas Archeological Survey,
The University of Texas at Austin

ASSEMBLAGE OF THE TOP LAYER AT FATE BELL. Materials of stone, shell, bone, antler, and wood are preserved. 1. fragment of basket 2. net 3. shell necklace 4. antler tool to chip flint 5. bone awls (tools used for making small holes in leather or wood) 6. stone arrowhead 7. wooden throwing stick 8. sandal 9. stone hand ax

Artifacts

Artifacts that are uncovered at archaeological sites are made up of materials that were available in the period in which they were made. The collection of artifacts found at a site is called an "assemblage."

But the further that archaeologists go back into the past, the less they find, as most materials—after a certain time—decay in the soil. A good example of the kinds of materials that are left from various time periods is found in the excavation of the Fate Bell shelter in southwest Texas, a very dry area that is most favorable for preservation. At this site archaeologists recently unearthed the remains of three different peoples living probably very much the same way of life—but belonging to different time periods.

Texas Archaeological Survey,
The University of Texas at Austin

Left: ASSEMBLAGE OF THE SECOND LAYER AT FATE BELL. Only the hard materials are preserved—stone, shell, bone, and antler. 1. stone arrowhead 2. stone hand ax 3. antler tool 4. shell from kitchen refuse 5. bone point

Above: ASSEMBLAGE OF THE THIRD LAYER AT FATE BELL. Only the two hardest mineral materials remain—stone and shell. 1. stone hand ax 2. stone arrowhead 3. shell from kitchen refuse

How Sites and Artifacts Are Dated

The method of radiocarbon dating helps archaeologists find out the age of ancient remains. The age of an artifact found at a given site indicates the age of all other artifacts found in the same stratum.

Charcoal is one of the most significant clues. Charcoal is a product of carbonized wood and remains preserved for great lengths of time. Thus pieces of charcoal are often found in excavations—either in hearths or in the timber remains of burned houses. Physicists can measure the amount of radioactivity, the giving off of radiocarbon atoms, left in the charcoal pieces and calculate the age of the sample.

Radiocarbon, or carbon 14, is a form of carbon that is tested to find out how old artifacts are. The method of testing is based upon the fact that trees, the original source of the charcoal, receive a certain amount of radiocarbon atoms from the air—as do all living things. The radiocarbon is absorbed by the tissues of the tree as long as it lives, although the atoms are continually disintegrating and new ones being received. When the tree dies, the carbon 14 atoms begin to disintegrate at a known and constant rate. The number of rays given off can be measured by a Geiger counter. In about 5,750 years, one half of the carbon 14 atoms are radiated. (Thus, carbon 14 is said to have a half-life of 5,750 years.) At a uniform rate the remainder of the radiocarbon is given off in the years that follow.

The age of any once-living, preserved object—up to about 40,000 years old—may be calculated by the radiocarbon method.

Above: **A PRESENT-DAY EXCAVATED AREA DI-
VIDED INTO A GRID. The grid is set in place
with a system of strings stretched upon large nails.**

Left: **THE "TREASURE HUNT" OF THE PAST.**
This is an example of excavation as it should not
be done. The careless methods of uncovering site
and artifacts date this picture as much as the
models of the automobiles.

Archaeologists at Work in the Field

When the first excavations took place, archaeologists
were mainly interested in collecting curios, and the expeditions were like treasure hunts. Today, an expedition
is scientific, and the work usually involves from ten to
twenty archaeologists. The area to be excavated is divided
into equal squares in a grid pattern. This is done to organize the excavation into separate sections and to be
able to systematically identify the exact locations where
artifacts are found.

R. H. Meadow

WORKMEN AT AN ARCHAEOLOGICAL SITE IN THE NEAR EAST.
Mohammed, the pickman, a worker, and Reza, the shovelman, enjoy posing
with the archaeologist's most important tools.

Each archaeologist is given a number of squares in
the marked-off area to excavate. Villagers are hired, some
as pickmen to loosen the dirt, some as workmen to fill up
the baskets and carry dirt out of the trenches, and some
as siftmen to sift the dirt and look for small objects that
might otherwise escape notice.

When an archaeological site is uncovered, the surface layer is first scraped in even, five-inch deep levels. The archaeologist's favorite tools are the trowel and the brush. For excavation of a Sumerian mound, for instance, the tip of the trowel is used to try to spot house foundations. The foundations are harder than the dirt-fill around them and can be located by lightly tapping the ground with the tip of the trowel. When the archaeologist locates the foundation, he has found the track, the direction the work will take. He then exposes the wall stumps, usually preserved to a height of one or two feet, and follows the directions the walls take within the trench. He carefully clears the area until the house floor is reached.

SIFTMEN. Small objects such as figurines, beads, rodent bones, and teeth are usually found on the screens.

Texas Archeological Survey,
The University of Texas at Austin

Texas Archeological Survey,
The University of Texas at Austin

TROWEL AND BRUSH. The edges of the trowel are used to scrape the walls and floor of the trench level. The point of the trowel is used to tap the ground around artifacts which appear. The brush is then used to re-move the dirt covering the artifacts.

WALL FOUNDATIONS AT THE SITE OF JARMO, IRAQ. Jarmo was a small village of about twenty houses. It was inhabited around 8,700 years ago by some of the earliest farmers of the world. Carbonized grains in their hearths showed that wheat and barley were cultivated. Large mortars and pestles were used to pound the cereals into a kind of porridge. Bones found in the kitchen refuse indicate that the people of Jarmo had domesticated goats and sheep.

The Oriental Institute, University of Chicago

Artifacts are usually found resting upon the plastered or beaten-earth floors. The objects are carefully exposed with a trowel or brush, but they are left <u>in situ</u>, the Latin term for "in place," until they are photographed.

After walls, floors, and artifacts are cleared, the archaeologist studies them as he would the pieces of a puzzle. Solving the puzzle will create a picture of the life that was once lived in the buried village. The shape and size of the houses that once stood at the site are indicated by

OBJECTS "IN SITU." The artifacts were completely exposed and then photographed in their original position.

Left: Arrowheads
Right: A celt

Texas Archeological Research Laboratory,
The University of Texas at Austin

 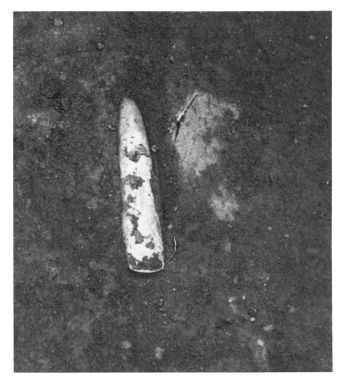

RESTORED HOUSE. The house was modeled from a foundation uncovered at the site of Jarmo and shown in the photograph on page 29. It was a small house, built of packed mud with a roof of brush and mud. There were two rectangular rooms lighted with small openings in the walls. The wooden framed door, dressed with skin or matting, opened into an enclosed court-yard where much of the family life must have been spent.

the contour of the walls; models can be reconstructed, as in the photograph below. The way of life of the former inhabitants is suggested by the tools that are found. In Jarmo, the finding of many sickle blades, and mortars and pestles suggested that the people were farmers culti-vating cereals. We have to use our imagination to visu-alize what a family meal in this house of long ago may have looked like. What do you think they may have talked about? What hopes and fears were they likely to have had?

Texas Archeological Survey,
The University of Texas at Austin

STONE ARROWHEADS. How many types of arrowheads can you see in this photograph? From all of the different styles, archaeologists can identify the people to whom they belonged and also the period at which they were made.

An abundance of spear and arrowheads found at a site indicates that the area was once the campsite of hunters. Archaeologists have even found, mixed with the ashes of the fireplace, the bones of the wild game eaten by the hunters during their last meal at the camp. Had we been there and shared this meal with them, what exciting stories we might have heard!

Uncovering the clues and trying to understand what life must have been like at a site are only parts of the archaeologist's task. He must also make available to others all of the information he has gathered. All artifacts are described in detail and are mapped on graph paper to show location and depth of the finding within the square. Many photographs are taken. Precise notes are made on the progress of work in each square, including all changes of color and consistency in the soil.

Texas Archeological Survey,
The University of Texas at Austin

Left: RECORDING. The floor of the site is completely uncovered. Before removing the artifacts, the archaeologist maps the exact position of each find on graph paper. The grid helps to measure the exact position of each artifact in the square.

Below: EXCAVATING BONES OF WILD GAME AT A SITE ONCE OCCUPIED BY HUNTERS. The excavator is applying a solution to the bones to solidify them. All of the bones can then be removed and sent to the zoological laboratory for identification and analysis.

Texas Archeological Survey,
The University of Texas at Austin

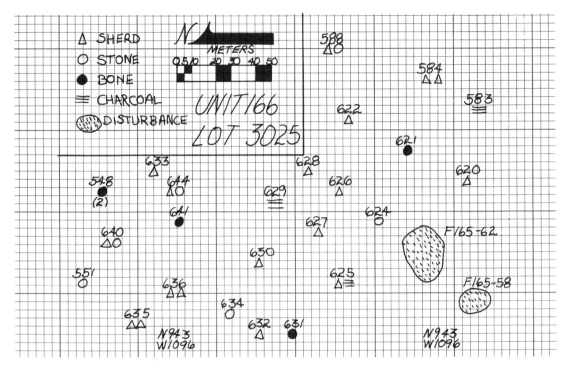

Texas Archeological Research Laboratory,
The University of Texas at Austin

Above: AN EXAMPLE OF A PAGE FROM AN ARCHAEOLOGIST'S NOTEBOOK. The mapping of a section of a trench is drawn on graph paper. The archaeologist has noted the number of the area excavated, the directions, and the scale of the map. Each number represents the field number received by each artifact excavated. Pottery is indicated by a triangle, bone by a dot, stone by a circle, and charcoal by three parallel horizontal strokes. The black areas indicated as "disturbances" may be pits dug from upper levels—or simply rodent holes.

Texas Archeological Survey,
The University of Texas at Austin

Right: PHOTOGRAPHING. Photographs and maps are the most valuable records kept by the archaeologist of the areas he has excavated. They are necessary for a study of the material and to present the evidences in publications.

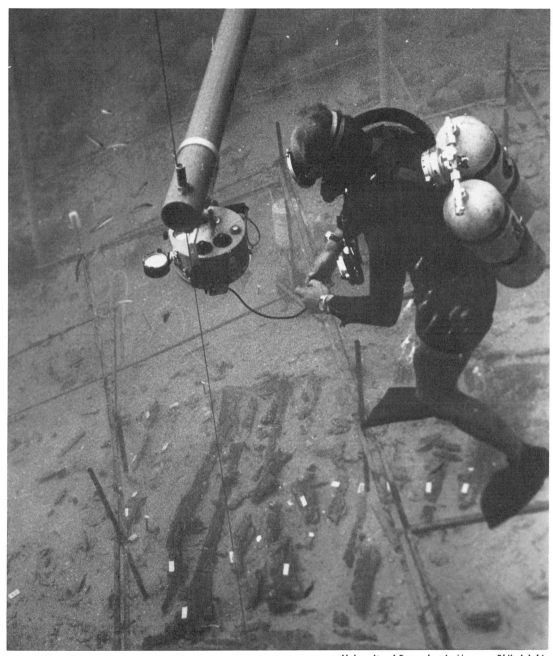

UNDERWATER PHOTOGRAPHY. Methods of recording, mapping, and photographing are also used by underwater archaeologists.

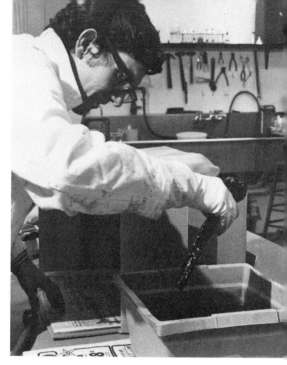

Texas Archeological Research Laboratory,
The University of Texas at Austin

CLEANING AND RESTORING ARTIFACTS. A spike belonging to a Spanish galleon of the sixteenth century was found incrusted with hard, chalky material, shells, and barnacles (animals with shells that attach themselves to rocks and the bottoms of ships). The method of electrolysis (i-lek-*trol*-uh-sis), the use of an electric current to break up chemical compounds, is used in the laboratory to clean off such objects. A preservative coating of wax is finally applied.

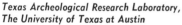

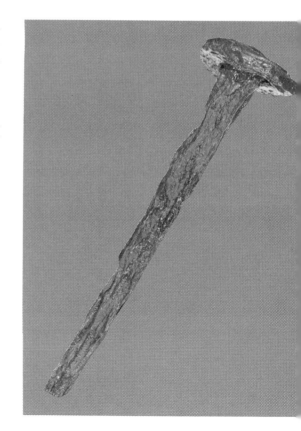

Texas Archeological Survey,
The University of Texas at Austin

BISON BONES IN SITU. Great accumulation of bones was found, among which pelvis, jaws, and ribs are easiest to recognize. All of the bones belonged to bisons, some of them having large fractures that might have been caused by a fall. In the photograph on page 38, locate the area in which the bones were found.

An Archaeological Puzzle

After having read about archaeologists and their work, you too can solve puzzles left to us from ancient times. Here is an archaeological problem for you.

At the foot of a high cliff, excavators unearthed a thick archaeological layer containing a large amount of piled-up bison bones. Among the bones were found two kinds of human tools, arrowheads and rough hand axes. Look carefully at the photograph on page 38. What do you think might have happened at this site long ago?

THE SITE. The archaeological layers were found in the area indicated by the arrow, just below the recess in the cliff.

Texas Archeological Survey,
The University of Texas at Austin

Above: **ROUGH HAMMER STONES FOUND WITH THE BONES.** Could these stones have been used to finish off the kill?

Texas Archeological Survey,
The University of Texas at Austin

Left: **ARROWHEADS.** One of these arrowheads was found "in situ," stuck between the ribs of a bison.

This photograph on page 41 is a reconstruction of the kill site shown on page 38. After studying all of the "puzzle" pictures, how do you think this environment affected the life of early people? What methods were used to kill buffalo, and why were they used? What do the weapons found at the site tell you about the people and their way of life?

If you could solve the puzzle left in the archaeological layers shown in these photographs, you are becoming an amateur archaeologist. From the study of site and artefacts, you were able to draw a picture of the past.

The Texas Memorial Museum,
The University of Texas at Austin

Right: RECONSTRUCTION OF A KILL SITE. Note the models of small figures. What are they doing? What is the purpose of the piled-up brush?

R. H. Meadow

Denise Schmandt-Besserat, Photographed at a Harvard Survey in Kerman, Iran.

ARCHAEOLOGY by Denise Schmandt-Besserat is an introduction to the subject of how archaeologists study early people and ancient civilizations. A graduate of Paris University and Ecole du Louvre, the author is presently an Assistant Professor in the College of Fine Arts at The University of Texas at Austin. She has been a Radcliffe Fellow, 1969-1971, and was a Research Fellow in Near Eastern Archaeology at the Peabody Museum, Harvard University. Her experiences in archaeological expeditions and her intense interest in the subject bring a fresh and vigorous spirit to the study of ancient times.